SELECTED POEMS
Henrik Nordbrandt

Augustinus/Curbstone

Some of these translations first appeared
in *Modern Poetry in Translation* and *Poets On.*
"Sailing" was originally published as a
Curbstone Press Poetry Broadside.

Cover lithograph by Niels Strøbek.

This publication was supported by a grant
from the National Endowment for the Arts
in Washington, D.C., a Federal Agency

and a grant from
the Connecticut Commission on the Arts

Curbstone Press also wishes to thank the following
agencies for their generous support:
Augustinus Foundation
Danish Ministry of Culture
Danish Ministry of Foreign Affairs
Scandinavia Today

1982: SECOND PRINTING
©1978 Alexander Taylor and Henrik Nordbrandt

LC: 78-1047
ISBN: 0-915306-33-6
Danish ISBN: 87-87710-10-2

distributed in Denmark by
Vindrose Forlag
14 Nybrogade
1203 Copenhagen K

AUGUSTINUS/CURBSTONE
321 Jackson Street
Willimantic, CT 06226

FOREWORD

When Henrik Nordbrandt called from New York City last August, I was delighted to hear his voice again, and I urged him and his wife, Anneli, to visit us in Willimantic. I well remembered admiring Henry's poems in Danish, and being deeply moved by the power of their imagery, their distinctive style, their assured idiomatic speaking voice, and their ability to portray unique moods. Nadia Christensen and I had already each translated some of his poems and had made some translations in collaboration. I looked forward with pleasure to the visit.

The few days' visit turned into a translating marathon of nearly two weeks. Somehow we just fell into it. And it was hardly work at all. I cannot really explain the excitement of a total collaboration in translation, but it is like the excitement of the creative process itself. It seemed to communicate itself to everyone around. Anneli, taking time out from her work on her dissertation, would type up the drafts and make excellent suggestions for changes. Judy Doyle, Pat Taylor, and Jim Scully also all made valuable recommendations. Each morning Henrik and I would revise the previous day's drafts and then go on to new ones. In less than two weeks, except for minor revisions, the book was finished. We at Curbstone feel fortunate that Henrik and Anneli were coaxed into visiting us here, not only because it gave us the benefit of their good companionship, but also because it gave Curbstone Press the opportunity to present the debut of Henrik's poetry to English and American audiences.

At the age of thirty-two, Henrik has already earned a permanent place in Danish letters. His first book of poems appeared when he was twenty-one, and in the eleven years since then he has published nine volumes of poetry. During these years he was fortunate enough to receive a number of small grants from the Danish government, and he lived in Greece and Turkey where, his money going further, he could devote himself entirely to writing. He is an admirer of Cavafy, one of the strongest individual voices in modern Greek literature, and Yumus Emre, the mystical Turkish poet of the Middle Ages, and though he is in no way imitative of either poet, he utilizes the strengths of both—an idiomatic, muscular speaking voice, and a blend of the concrete and the mystical:

> I have squandered my money on roses, I have lost my way
> in blue.
> If I don't see you tomorrow I am a dead man
> lying far out at sea under a pale March sky
>
> like a phantom ship that has outsailed its figurehead
> and left its reflection in all the windows
> with a rose in one hand, and the other outstretched
> and open.

Danish reviewers have been quick to recognize his immense talent. Bettina Heltberg, writing in *Politiken* (11-23-77), said: "Every poem Henrik Nordbrandt has written bears, as in the work of all great masters, his unmistakable signature: the definitive unity of motif and style."

In Henrik Nordbrandt's poetry we hear a clear direct speaking voice which often evokes unusual moods and startling psychic directions with an energy which conjures up in us memories of indefinable experience:

> At midnight, in my sleep, I was invaded by ants
> that carried me up over the mountains
> and onto the plateaus beyond, toward new mountains ...
>
> At dawn I awoke as a constellation
> in a well, a figure drinking
> its cool waters from hands that had forsaken him.
>
> ("Constellation")

His is also a voice that can range from the nightmarish dislocation portrayed in "Guerilla Death Certificate" to the sheer lyric joy of "To Sleep in Your Arms."

Since Henrik travels extensively and has lived for ten years in Turkey and Greece, it is not unusual that we find references in his poems to such places as Baglama, Athens, Ithaca, Baklava, Byzantium, Denizli . . . but these are not so much literary references as they are signposts and places encountered by a traveller who is seeking for something even he himself does not fully understand:

> No matter where we go, we always arrive too late
> to experience what we left to find
>
> ("No Matter Where We Go")

6

"Late Summer" concludes:

> [I] walk further, more weary, burdened by a new loss
> without quite knowing where I've come from
> or what it is I've sought so much I've lost it.

This sense of loss, however, does not predominate in all the poems. In "Going Ashore," for instance, the seeker, "after so many futile travels," suddenly experiences again "each word as a declaration of love." This poem ends:

> I worship the burning earth because it forces me to dance
> and my worn-out masks because they force me to laugh.
> I worship my indifferent death because it forces me to live.

With characteristic energy, these lines convey Henrik's belief in the grace of affliction as well as his healthy humorous self-perspective. Perhaps that is why even his saddest poems are not ultimately depressing. You have a sense that the balance is being maintained, the quest continues, and the quester has grown wiser and stronger.

No discussion of Henrik Nordbrandt would be complete without mentioning his love poetry—he has written some of the most interesting, most lyrical, and most modern love poems of our time. Poems such as "Now I Can No Longer Use You" and "Sailing" express with wit and originality a profoundly felt love which clearly recognizes the essential otherness and integrity of the beloved:

> Now I can no longer use you
> as a rose in my love poems:
> you are much too large, much too beautiful
> and much, too much yourself.

> ("Now I Can No Longer Use You")

In "Sailing" each of the lovers is symbolized as a ship, each maintaining its separate identity, although they are delightfully together,

> —without one of them ever trying
> to outsail the other
> and without the distance between them
> lessening or growing at all.

Perhaps Henrik is essentially a love poet. Throughout his work you feel his love for places, for people, for words, for experience, and even for adversity, the burning earth that teaches him to dance.

—Alexander Taylor
Willimantic, Connecticut
January 5, 1978

CONTENTS

I

II

III

IV

V

I

CHINA OBSERVED THROUGH
GREEK RAIN
IN TURKISH COFFEE

The drizzle
falls into my coffee
until it gets cold
and runs over
until it runs over
and clears
so the picture at the bottom
comes into sight.

The picture of a man
with a long beard
in China
in front of a Chinese pavillion
in rain, heavy rain
that has congealed
in stripes
over the windblown facade
and over the face of the man.

Under the coffee, the sugar and the milk
which is curdling
under the worn glaze
the eyes seem burnt out
or turned inward
toward China, in the porcelain of the cup
slowly emptying of coffee
and running full of rain
clear rain. The spring rain

atomizes against the eaves of the tavern
the facades on the other side of the street
resemble a huge
worn wall of porcelain
whose glow penetrates the wine leaves
the wine leaves which are also worn
as if inside a cup. The Chinaman
sees the sun appear through a green leaf
which has fallen into the cup

the cup whose contents
are now completely clear.

AEGEAN SEA

Aegean Sea, it was your waves
which in the hot summer nights
lifted me up to my sleeping face
to the crumbling statues'
confidential kisses on my forehead
to my fingertips which suddenly remembered
the eyelids of sailors' widows
and the gold of fading icons
and to my veins which were shattered within me
like fragile glass in a Roman
grave in Central Asia. And only the salt
from the underwater grottoes you dug in my dreams
and from the ships I weighted down
struggling to be one with you
let me recognize myself
when in sleep I stroked a face
whose large, open eyes, distended nostrils and billowing beard
I believed must belong to another.

CHASE

Borne onward by the dreams of drunken sailors, I kiss again
    the Aegean Sea: like a figurehead on their ship
with the sunset in my face, subjected to their will.
    What do they want of me? Where are they dreaming me to?
Each of them is dreaming about me, each of them madly desires
    my naked, salt-spattered body in his dreams.
And together, full of hate, they drive me onward through the night.

They chase me through harbors they have plundered to no purpose
    and with slivers of broken glass force me to dance.
And while I dance for them amid jeers and obscene gestures
    I bear them forward over the sea, forward
on a slimy deck where their bodies roll, abandoned
    in brackish water, puke and blood and wine and tar
held together by a hull sighing in its joints.

They dream of splintering me with axes, limb by limb
    of crushing my eyes under their salt lids
and my lips which sun and seawater have almost completely eaten away.
    Driven onward by their will I bear them onward
just to crush the ship beneath them, to kiss them to their death
    against the cliffs which their dreams raise from the sea
desolate and rugged, through foam-crested waves at daybreak.

TONIGHT

Tonight I am tired enough
to sleep in the prisons
and in the river beds
under the snow-clad mountains
and I can sink with the ships
chained to the galley thwarts
in the flower scent under Africa's coasts.
Tonight I am tired enough
to make my grave beautiful
with tormented memories
which become mine only
as bit by bit I forget them.
Tonight I can trace
my veins all the way out
until things go black.
And the weight of my skeleton
will tell me tonight
the height of the mountain passes
I go beyond in my dreams.

"NAXOS", "SAPPHO", "KNOSSOS"

One trivial day
follows the other
"Naxos" of Naxos
sails to Naxos
"Sappho" of Lesbos
to Lesbos
and "Knossos" of Heraklion
to Heraklion
all three of them from Piraeus
and back again, each day.

Oh, blue Aegean Sea.

On Naxos I miss
the roses on Lesbos
on Lesbos the mountains on Crete
and on Crete I miss
every connection
between the three islands.

Oh, I wish I could be aboard
all three ships at the same time.
Or I wish that "Naxos"
would stop at Lesbos
on its way to Crete
and that "Sappho" would stop at Heraklion
on its way to Naxos.
I wish "Knossos" would sail
directly to Sappho.

What the hell do I mean?

Oh, blue Aegean Sea
your islands disjoint me
so I get drunk between them.
"Naxos" of Naxos
sails to Naxos
"Sappho" of Lesbos
to Lesbos
and "Knossos" of Heraklion
to Heraklion
all three from Piraeus
and back again, each day.

On their decks the loudspeakers blare
the same tunes, each day
while the passengers drink rum and coke
or ouzo on the rocks
staring out over the sea
slowly collapsing
from boredom over their tall glasses.

Oh, "Naxos", "Sappho" and "Knossos"
you disjoint my life.
My desperation
is your longing for one another.

One trivial day
follows the other.
I die of longing
in noisy Piraeus
far away from Naxos
far away from Lesbos
far away from Heraklion
far away from Sappho
far away from Dionysos
far away from Appollon
far away from Ariadne

or on board "Naxos"
of longing for Lesbos
on board "Sappho"
of longing for Crete
or on board "Knossos"
of longing for Naxos.

Oh, Sappho
take me with you to Knossos.
Oh, Ariadne
liberate me from my prison on Naxos.
Oh, Dionysos
sail me away from Appollon.
Fall, Ikaros
fall, for Christ's sake.

For I'm drunk, drunk I say
as never before.

I dream of putting
the roses from Lesbos
on the mountains of Crete
and seeing them glow in the sunlight
from the coast of Naxos . . . .

I dream of a ship
called "Naxos" of Lesbos
or "Sappho" of Naxos.
I long for "Knossos" of Sappho
"Lesbos" of Heraklion
Ariadne of Naxos
Dionysos of the Blue
"Appollon" of Everywhere
and Ikaros of Nowhere.

Oh, handsome, impossible ships
why don't you exist?

I have seen Sappho
from the deck of "Naxos"
and "Naxos"
from the deck of "Knossos"
and "Knossos"
from the deck of "Sappho".
And that's all
they sailed past each other.

Each of them reminded me
in her special way
of my life
which is disjointed a little, each day
and returns to itself again
with the same intolerable precision.

BAGHLAMA

When he got up, staggering a little
and began to dance to the music of the juke box
the others ceased their conversations
and started to clap their hands, bang the tables
and smash their glasses on the filthy cement floor
in time with the rising rhythm. Faster
and faster he whirled about in the smoke-filled room
on naked feet among heaps of broken glass
till the sweat-glistening faces and the light of the taverna
disappeared around him. The dark streets outside
lead him out of himself through their labyrinths
and further on across the dusty open squares in the moonlight
through the dilapidated suburbs and farther out into the night.
Before long he was aboard the ships
on his way into the dawn. The smells and voices
of Iskenderun, Beirut and Alexandria rose about him.
Simultaneously he went ashore in ten different harbors
and was at the same time ten different men
who had disembarked at the same place and had gotten drunk there.
Dizzy he looked upon his own bleeding body
through the eyes of his friends when they bent over him,
seized him and threw him out onto the street
among skinny dogs, wailing women and grimy children.
Then the next one rose and began to dance
to the hoarse cheers of the others and the sound of breaking glass.
Around them their surroundings disappeared.
They whirled out into the night, scattering in all directions
like dancing reflections of a dancer
who sees himself everywhere as everybody and nobody.

GOING ASHORE

After so many futile travels, after so many attempted escapes
without precisely knowing what it was I was looking for
without conviction, without charts and carried forward by sinking ships
after having described the things I saw again and again
so many times that they ceased to exist as anything but words
—after so many empty phrases and so many gratuitous lies
suddenly I experience again each word as a declaration of love.

And I worship each word because it forces me to sing
the way we sing in praise of storms at sea
because they force us to submit to them and seek refuge
in so many unknown harbors on so many enchanted islands.
I worship the cities where we were beaten up, for their names
the black olives, the bread, and the word for wine in seven languages.
I worship the countries we never saw because they forced us to invent ther

I worship the burning earth because it forces me to dance
and my worn-out masks because they force me to laugh.
I worship my indifferent death because it forces me to live.

ATHENS

We have been travelling so long
we no longer know where we live.
But if we did know
we would go straight home . . . .

We call this city Athens
but we really can't
have arrived in Athens yet
since this place corresponds neither with
our memories nor our imaginings.

And since it is not Athens
how can we leave again
as long as we do not know
what place it is we are leaving?

So let us stay here a while
take a look at the ruins and get to know the city
and if after a time
we begin to feel so much at ease
we are convinced that it is Athens

we can begin again
to wonder where we live
and at that time
hopefully go straight home . . . .

NO MATTER WHERE WE GO

No matter where we go, we always arrive too late
to experience what we left to find.
And in whatever cities we stay
it is the houses where it is too late to return
the gardens where it's too late to spend a moonlit night
and the women whom it's too late to love
that disturb us with their intangible presence.

And whatever streets we think we know
take us past the gardens we are searching for
whose heavy fragrance spreads throughout the neighborhood.
And whatever houses we return to
we arrive too late at night to be recognized.
And in whatever rivers we look for our reflections
we see ourselves only when we have turned our backs.

THE HOMECOMING

Your parents
have become parents
to others
and your brothers and sisters, neighbors.
The neighbors
have become neighbors to others
and the others live
in other cities.
In the other cities they return
just like you.
And they find you
no more
than you find them.

PRAYER

I ask you by everything we have loved:

By the summer mornings when we awoke in foreign harbors
    which we could never have imagined
—with such well-being, such joy
    of not knowing what lay behind the mountains.—
I ask you by the harbors where the breeze is full of a spice revealing
    the presence of deserts and strange burial rites.
By the nights on the Mediterranean, where the sunken cities
    described by the crew in a language we scarcely understood
weighted us down like tears of gold we could not cry.
Yes, by all the chaotic languages which are spoken aboard
    the fishing boats at night—so full of euphony, so full of names.—
I ask you by the names of stones and gods in Greek,
    by the names of stars in Arabic
    and by the sweetness of the prolonged verb endings in Turkish.
By the sunrays in the underwater caves south of Harlicarnassos.
By the afternoon light in the wave crests which break on the port side
    when you sail eastward between Cyprus and Asia Minor.
I ask you by the wave crests which glitter like daydreams
    dreamt by deposed childless sultans in beds of mother-of-pearl.
By the beds of child brides which float up in the night like sails
    pulling an invisible ship whose crew has been dead for years
into the garden where the wounded partisans are hiding.
By the young widows of the partisans
    who bleed to death like pomegranates
crushed in ingenious jewelry boxes of gold and emeralds.
I ask you by the scent of fifteen-year-old girls
    in the Asian August night
    when the men fire their rifles in the public square
and for no apparent reason drop dead, their faces blue-black.
By the scent of decayed houses set on stilts in the misty estuaries
    where drunken old men come home late at night
to kill their melancholic daughters with broken bottles.
I ask you by the names of the houses
    where a hundred years always goes by
    from the time you go out in the evening

to the time you return in the morning.
By the houses in the blossoming almond groves
     under the snowcapped mountains.
I ask you by the blossoming almond trees which look like loves
   ended long ago without bitterness
and without memories to disturb the children before they go to sleep.
By the children who in the evening
     raise their rose and golden paper kites
   out over the violet sea.
I ask you by the violet sea, the violet sea in the foreign harbors
   the moment before we awaken.

I ask for everything that we have loved.

OSTRACHON

Greece, you have kissed me through and through
and left me as an imprint
of your archaic lips
                  on your sunbaked walls

Most clearly seen in the dark eyes
of the children, who have grown up during the time
that has passed since first
                  I tasted your bitter salt

and the longing for your being
that grew more and more unquenchable
the more I drank of it
                  the deeper into it I sank.

The hard toys of the sun in the surf:
the stones that want to burst the heart
which is opening and closing caressingly
                  around their angular shapes.

LATE SUMMERS

I come from late summers of vague melancholy
long as piano lessons in vacated suburbs
where the facades can no longer bear the darkness of the houses
and people have become ghosts in their own eyes.

Where the east wind ravages the yards like a madman
who scrapes his bones clean with a rusty knife
and falls to earth with a sound like Mongolia
and each sunlit wall concludes an entire century.

Where blue evenings sing empty wells through the heart
and each shadow is a trap door in a church
and where I overtake my waiting form on every corner

and walk further, more weary, burdened by a new loss
without quite knowing where I come from
or what it is I've sought so much I've lost it.

ON THE WAY TO ITHACA

On the way to Ithaca I see myself at last:
A shape more blurred with the crest of each wave
as the men who created
its cold blue contours by rowing the ship forward

gradually are left astern, perish in their dreams
or fall dead on the oars:
Their disappearance brings me, bit by bit,
to the arrival that has always pursued me:

Pink mountains, capped with snow, jutting
from a pink sea, dissolve my features in theirs.
I am the nobody Ithaca has made me.

The Ithaca mirrored in the sea I abandoned.
The Ithaca I thought was my longing
when that longing still had a form and could be stilled.

AEGINA

It is a word for despair that cannot be expressed
which shatters the world no matter what we sing.
It is no afternoon stifling itself with roses
and no figure seven, no mask of gold.
It has no mouth, and no sex. No daughters
and it is not blue like the walls of September.
It does not see its reflection hung beneath burned wings
on the way to Byzantium. And the name Aegina
whispered in an empty cistern does not make it sob.
When we dream of it like a ship
which we are rowing toward a dark, rocky coast
to meet ourselves as doubles risen in salt,
we know it's a lie yet keep on rowing
singing wildly to the metronome's quickening beat.

WATCH

After seven days of unbroken rain
on the evening of the seventh day
the wet stones on the shore
are the only usable lamps.

Those that stay with us
when the ships have sunk
the rotten houses fallen down
and the terraces washed into the sea.

When we lift them up in our hands
and stare into the darkness
we see ourselves standing as guards

posted behind the walls of a foreign city
whose inhabitants have fled:
The wind blows upon us through its open gates.

TROY

Each day I am someone different than the day before
and day by day I move further into darkness:
Before me is a long line of people I have been —
those nearest, still wrapped in twilight,
those farther away, in the light, casting shadows
and the farthest ones, wholly transparent
like the husks of insects or rock-crystal statues
fallen forward or completely apart
exposing their hidden flaws and defects.
Those I will become stand behind me:
a line of figures equally dark, equally vague —
I do not know how long it is —
clumsy, struggling, half-conscious bodies
waiting to take my place.
Each day I am someone different, and each day the same:
The figure in the middle that blocks the view
keeping those ahead from understanding
the wild energy and longing for light of those behind,
and keeping those behind from learning
from the flaws and failings of those ahead.
I am Helen, and at the same, the Hellenes
the rowers who row the carved prows into daybreak
and each separate rower who, chained to his oar,
rows with the feeling of never getting anywhere at all.

HEADLONG FALL

Asia, your hot August nights
ignite themselves around me
like widows who cannot survive
the loss of my lean body

which, lifeless, rising and falling
in the well of their seething dreams
gradually loses its surroundings
and becomes aware of its own weight

like a statue of polished basalt
that sinks into an awareness
of being unaware and set free.
Set free from the wounded bodies

that cling to me in the darkness
from the blood that moistens my stoneflesh
from the flames that shatter me
and from the dreams that created me.

BAKLAVA

I feel uneasy in Athens, Istanbul,
and also in Beirut. People there
seem to know something about me
which I myself never understood,
something enticing and dangerous
like the submerged necropolis
where we dove for amphorae last summer,
a secret — half perceived
when touched by the street vendors' glances
suddenly makes me painfully aware
of my skeleton. As if the gold coins
the children hold out toward me
were stolen from my own grave
last night. As if casually they
had crushed every bone in my head
to get at them. As if
the cake I just ate
were sweetened with my own blood.

BYZANTIUM

Woodsmoke drifts away over the sunken graves
    and the winter evening's waning light
reaches a limit where only the faces of the condemned
    are strong enough to muster sufficient resistance.
Women calling out into the darkness from the open doors
    of dilapidated houses try to tell me something
which the children, who reluctantly interrupt their games
    in the ruins of the church, do not understand.
And throughout the night black stallions with bloodshot eyes
    run wild in the narrow streets
when, from the sound of their hoofbeats, they sense that
    the riders in the silver-studded saddles died a long time ago.

POSTCARD WITH ANGELS

The three wisemen from the East
having forgotten what they came for
stand bewildered on the hill above the town.
Winter does not need their features
to model its deathmask on.

And the whiteness is complete without them.
They have become its fellow readers;
guided by an obliterated handwriting
they travel toward their own shining statues
in a world transformed into a mausoleum.

Where we stand, each in front of his entrance
trying to forget it —
through that village twilight
an ever colder awakening
turns the folds of our clothing to stone.

Clouds of peat smoke swirl through the air
and fall slowly onto the snow:
Even the angels become visible, and grey —
the angels who look at us
with the same expression as the drunken soldiers

and the three wisemen up on the hill.

TO CAPTURE BYZANTIUM

At times, and from far away, you must capture Byzantium
—to drive the Byzantine blood from your veins
to free yourself from your Byzantine limbs:
The tired, outstretched wings on which in dark dreams you glide
through tunnels and rugged mountain passes,
all the shining metal that weighs down your ivory arms
and the perfumes that eat away your heavy eyelids—
It is Byzantium you must capture in order to master them.

To capture Byzantium is a task for dreamers.
Only dreamers will be able to choose the right time
the instant between night and day when the city is immersed
in the golden light which makes the dreamers invisible
and is reflected on the secret gates built by the dreamers.
Only dreamers, in their deepest sleep, can discover the openings
from which their blood longs to flow
and the gold their limbs long to be free of.

At times, and from far away, you must capture Byzantium
—to be able to drive yourself from Byzantium
to lead yourself past yourself with its streets
to make yourself a stranger against its strange bodies
to become an object of its intrigues
to have your face removed from its icons
to taste your bones with its sunken graves.
It is Byzantium you must capture in order to free yourself.

OUR LOVE IS LIKE BYZANTIUM

Our love is like Byzantium
must have been
on the last evening. There must have been
I imagine
a glow on the faces
of those who crowded the streets
or stood in small groups
on streetcorners and public squares
speaking together in low voices
that must have resembled
the glow your face has
when you brush your hair back
and look at me.

I imagine they haven't spoken
much, and about rather
ordinary things
that they have been trying to say
and have stopped
without having managed to express
what they wanted
and have been trying again
and given up again
and have been looking at each other
and lowered their eyes.

Very old icons, for instance
have that kind of glow
the blaze of a burning city
or the glow which approaching death
leaves on photographs of people who died young
in the memory of those left behind.

When I turn towards you
in bed, I have a feeling
of stepping into a church
that was burned down long ago
and where only the darkness in the eyes of the icons
has remained
filled with the flames
which annihilated them.

FUNERAL PORTRAIT

In wonder, we held you up in the sunlight
and wiped the dust from your face.
With the expression of a wounded traveller
who one spring day just at evening
arrives at a little village in the mountains
and dies, without having been able to say
who he is, and where he comes from
— thus your image spoke to us.
Your mouth tried to express something
we ourselves had always wanted to say
and your eyes observed a landscape
we ourselves had always longed for.

As if the uncertainty of your fate
with those you left long ago
and the uncertainty of your genesis
with those who laid you in your grave
made you an object for a surmise
whose unformulated, half-guessed words
united the first with the last in us
when once again we held you up in the light.
And when we wiped the dust from your face
we didn't know who it was
who touched you with our hands:
Whether it was those whom you left
who again caressed you, in longing
or whether it was those whom you died among
who again touched your corpse, in anxiety.

— All that we knew, O traveller
was that we felt compelled to destroy you again.
And like the soldiers who left you behind
wounded in the mountains, we wounded you once again
with broken bottles and fag-ends of cigarettes
before we shattered you with our rifle butts
and burned down the chapel we found you in.

CHORA

The days move their walls through the town.
The white walls become fewer and fewer,
their light more and more intense.
The blue walls become more and more numerous.

Wall by wall we move with them . . .
till we have lived in all the houses
followed all the streets to their end
and come out on the other side

where all walls are blue and covered with stars
where before there were roses in the sunshine.

ON THE PLAIN

The first, light clouds
on the blue sky

cast heavy shadows
on the tall, yellow grass.

To cry is just as hard
as it feels easy.

AUTUMN MOUNTAINSIDES

Autumn mountainsides in afternoon sun
and the rest of the landscape deep in shadow
covered by a thin layer of frost.
Only the pebbles of the river can still shine
through the reflection of the clear sky.

Sounds come from a distant country
that has no name, until finally they come
with a suddenness of horsehooves
when the riders have ridden away again
and taken half of us with them.

OCTOBER 20, 1971

Tonight it snowed on the Taurus Mountains
far in the distance
across the strait
and now the cool air
has made them visible
for the first time
in four months, I think.

The few tourists
left on the beach
seem a little cold
and the noise of crammed paper-bags
and cigarette packets
occasionally moving
half buried in sand
seems so unnaturally loud.

The scene resembles
Scott Fitzerald
after he had written
"The Great Gatsby"
and before he
began to drink in earnest.

At a time
when he probably knew
how the whole act was going to end.

WHEN A PERSON DIES

When a person dies
his surroundings remain behind:

The mountains in the distance
the neighborhood houses
and the road that on Sunday
leads over a wooden bridge
on the way out of town.

And the spring sunshine
that rather late in the afternoon
reaches a shelf of books
and magazines which undoubtedly
were once new.

It's not a bit strange.

But all the same it has
often surprised me.

TO A DEATH MASK

You are a child of your own sleep and therefore sleepless.
For your sake wanderers on the glass-mountain slope never
find rest, the bird never finds its way back to its nest
and the wind in the prayer-wheel repeats your words in a ceaseless
cradle-song that keeps you awake. You are set like a door
in the opening which dreamers go through when they awaken
but through which you yourself are never allowed to pass,
You are a child of those who sleep and for their sake eternally sleepless.

GERMAN SOLDIERS' GRAVES

Now the skeletons lie exposed
on the border between mould and clay, like split
hearts in open wounds. If they still

beat, they are heard only by moles
by blind moles and insect larvae
hibernating for the winter.

And for the sake of your diary, Liebchen,
I note that the sun is about to go down. October
leaves fall, you would say, like a gentle funeral march.

But there is also another sound. Of earth
dropped down into earth, a resonance-box of earth
laid in circles of earth. Winds which understood nothing

have become their own answers. Reassuring:
a thin husk of bone
divides us from metaphysics.

CIVIL WAR

The moon cannot find
what it came to shine on.
Whitewash has flaked from the houses.
The riverbed has run dry.
And the young widows have forgotten
how to look up.

GUERILLA DEATH CERTIFICATE

There is a house somebody has left many years ago
there is a voice which has long since fallen silent
there is a certain place you must always return to
there is a spring full of cherry trees and poppy petals
there is a firing squad you're never allowed to see
there is a girl named Maria who could have no other name
there is a vase with violets a mirror and an old table
there is a place where nobody dares to see who has come
there has never been anyone to write a certain letter
there has never been a letter delivered to the person mentioned there
there has never been mention of a house which isn't there at all
there is no house you can leave when you are not there
there is no place to return to when you are nobody
there is nobody who could not have another name than Maria
there is no firing squad that cannot be forgotten
there is no shattered mirror to reflect the poppy petals
there is only a silent voice talking about everything which is
there is somebody who has left a house many years ago
there is a girl named Maria who could not have another name
there is a vase with violets a mirror and an old table
there is a firing squad you are never allowed to see
there is a house where you sit down without being there
there is a place where nobody dares to see who has come
there is a piece of paper where you write you are nobody

ASCENT TOWARD AKSEKI

1.

The snow that burdens
the branches of the blossoming almond trees
when it clears
after a brief flurry
makes the mountains hover.

2.

The song meant to be sung
in the mountains
refuses to be sung
any other place.
It would kill the singer.

3.

Death is a country
without mountains
that we climb on all fours.

4.

I approach the mountain
through blossoming almond groves.
I'm happy
that there's no other way.

5.

When ashes cover the mountain
it looks like a mountain of ashes.
When bones cover the mountain
it looks like a mountain of bones.
When thrushes cover the mountain
it looks like a mountain of thrushes.
When violets cover the mountain
all of a sudden it looks like a mountain.

MEDITATING CAMEL

The white snowcapped mountains out there
behind the spring-green steppes
give the steppes the character of steppes

and the spring-green steppes
on the other hand
give the mountains the character of mountains

so that the steppes become bounded and flat
and possible, therefore, to stand on
and watch the mountains from, as long

as the snow is covering them.

IV

TAURUS

I don't know which I prefer:
You, my love, over the Taurus mountains
or the Taurus mountains over roses

so beautiful are the Taurus mountains
so red and deeply fragrant are the roses.
Precisely so much do I love you.

AGORAPHILIA

You are my love and my despair.
You are my madness and my understanding.
And you are all the places where I have not been

that call to me from all the corners of the world.
You are these six lines
in which I must confine myself in order not to scream.

I HAVE SQUANDERED MY MONEY
ON ROSES

I have squandered my money on roses, I have lost my way in blue.
If I don't see you tomorrow I am a dead man
lying far out at sea under a pale March sky

like a phantom ship that has outsailed its figurehead
and left its reflection in all the windows
with a rose in one hand, and the other outstretched and open.

GOBI

Seven steps from spring, the questions become answers.
Your face from darkness the violets become dust.
Nine nights from the mountains. Thirteen mouths from insanity.

God masturbates us with his horrible mathematics.
The Gobi desert counts his cells by sand,
we by tears when we look into the sky of spring.

BODRUM

Who are you? Who are you? Who are you? Who are you?
Tell me before the winds of dawn
Tell me before the seven double locks rust shut.

The machines approach their enigmas with our blood
the poppy fields their distance with our bones.
Our bodies approach their impressions with museums.

CONSTELLATION

At midnight, in my sleep, I was invaded by ants
that carried me up over the mountains
and onto the plateaus beyond, toward new mountains . . .

At dawn I awoke as a constellation
in a well, a figure drinking
its cool waters from hands that had forsaken him.

KASTELORIZON

Of the sea from last summer
only the reflection of the sunset is left
of the reflection only the faces
and of the faces only their waiting.

MEMORY OF DENIZLI

A dance upon coals is this life
under the high blue sky of spring.
Only these four lines keep me from
casting myself out into it.

IT IS WINTER HERE

It is winter here: The mountains are covered with snow
and sounds travel faster than our thoughts.
Through the high, clear air I shout the name
of the place I do not know before I get an answer.

A LIFE

You struck a match and its flame blinded you
so you couldn't find what you were looking for in the darkness
before the match burned out between your fingers
and pain made you forget what you were looking for.

HEAD OF CLAY

The storm has washed a head of clay up on the shore.
It is a sea nymph
and from the relationship of the face to the neck
it seems she has something in her hand
she is fond of. She looks
most of all like a girl from the country on her way to a dance
but has something sad about her
which she can't explain.

Now you carefully scrape the chalk from her face
to try to find out
what it is that troubles her. She looks
as if she were sleeping, dreaming
in a meadow. But on her cheek
near the right corner of her mouth is
embedded in the clay a birthmark
which she is trying to hide under a tuft of hair.

It is shaped like the imprint of a finger
the little finger of the right hand
and put there long ago when you once
touched her, only once, to thank her
for something you no longer remember.
Maybe it was only that she yielded
to your wishes exactly the way you wanted, so beautiful
you couldn't bear to leave her alone.

STREETS

Loves that ended long ago:

Sometimes you meet them in the street
sometimes you meet them in dreams.

When you meet them in the street, they resemble dreams
when you meet them in dreams, they resemble streets

streets where half the houses are empty
because you don't remember whose faces

appear in the darkness behind the windows.

WHEN WE LEAVE EACH OTHER

When we leave each other, we also leave
all the places we have been together:

The neglected suburb with its smoke-stained houses
where we lived a month, towns where we spent a night
whose names we have forgotten, and stinking hotels in Asia
where we awoke occasionally in the heat of noon
feeling we had slept for a thousand and one years.

And all the tiny, nearly inaccessible mountain chapels
along the road from Athens to Delphi
where the oil lamps burn all through the summer night

we also leave when we leave each other.

TIBETAN DREAM

I saw a child sitting
on the shore of a sea

and thought it was my child
and wanted to go up to it

when it turned around
and shook its head

as if wishing to say:
Do not use me again

in your dreams: You are
dead and have no right

to murder yourself once more
by appearing here.

DAYS LATE IN MARCH

Days move in one direction
faces in the opposite.
Incessantly they lend each other light.

Many years later it is difficult
to decide which were days
and which were faces . . . .

And the distance between the two things
seems more impassable
day by day and face by face.

That is what I see on your face
these shining days late in March.

THE ROSE FROM LESBOS

I got this rose from an unknown woman
on my way into an unknown town.
— And now that I have been in the town
slept in its beds, played cards under its plane-trees

gotten drunk in its taverns
and seen the woman come and go and go and come
I no longer know where to throw it.

Everywhere I have been, its scent lingers
and everywhere I have not been
its withered petals lie crumpled in the dust.

SMILE

When I saw you in my dream
you turned towards me

with a finger on your lips
and raised eyebrows

smiling, before you continued
softly walking

through the neglected
moon-lit room

which I suddenly understood
was meant to represent my life.

SHADOWS

I have been thinking so much about you
and have written so much about you
without knowing precisely who you are.
I have slept in so many rooms
without having you at my side
and there are so many houses I have moved into
and out of again without you.
There are so many cities where I have not met you.

There are so many things I've worn out
or lost on my way to you,
and so many possibilities I have wasted,
so many lives, your presence, here and now,
makes me feel I have squandered,
so that now I can not see you as other than
the spring light that occasionally brushes your cheek
or makes the glow in your eye burst into flame

leaving the shadows doubly deep and cold.

TO SLEEP IN YOUR ARMS

To sleep in your arms
is every bit as curious and beautiful
as to be imperial
birdcatcher in a fairyland
where all things have wings
and fly back and forth among each other
because they think it's fun to fly
and because they love to be caught
and let loose again
so they really can enjoy their wings
their purple and silvery
and emerald green and golden wings
in the fabulous violet dusk
where you are lying beside me
like a starling that has fallen to earth
wet and ruffled, its feathers and eyelids
glued shut by the white poppyglue of sleep.

NOW I CAN NO LONGER USE YOU

Now I can no longer use you
as a rose in my love poems:
you are much too large, much too beautiful
and much, much too much yourself.

Now I can really only look at you
as one looks at a river
which has found its own bed
and enjoys it in each of its movements

each of its turns, each of its fish
and each of its sunsets
between the blue snowcapped mountains
which are mine and mine alone

because you have carved your way through them.
Now I can only mirror myself
in your calm flowing waters
along with the fallen petals of flowers

the barges and the deserted mining towns
where your lovers get drunk
and drown themselves in your moonshine
and are washed up on the banks

in the distant countries where we meet in our dreams.

SAILING

After having loved we lie close together
and at the same time with distance between us
like two sailing ships that enjoy so intensely
their own lines in the dark water they divide
that their hulls
are almost splitting from sheer delight
while racing, out in the blue
under sails which the night wind fills
with flowerscented air and moonlight
— without one of them ever trying
to outsail the other
and without the distance between them
lessening or growing at all.

But there are other nights, where we drift
like two brightly illuminated luxury liners
lying side by side
with the engines shut off, under a strange constellation
and without a single passenger on board:
On each deck a violin orchestra is playing
in honor of the luminous waves.
And the sea is full of old tired ships
which we have sunk in our attempt to reach each other.

LITTLE MORNING PRAYER

The saddest thing in the world
is a candle

burning in the sunshine
in early morning

after the night of love
it illuminated so beautifully.

O God let our love
never become like that.

DISSERTATION

While you are writing your dissertation on Danish art
and I find it indiscreet to mention precisely
  which period it covers
I am thinking of Zafer, which means victory,
  and her 14-15 year old daughter, Seher
which means dawn, and I don't know which of them
  I love the most
but that the spring evening has never been more beautiful,
  that I know.
Seher goes to the well for water,
  and to avoid meeting her penetrating eyes
I seek refuge in a poem by Heine, which has the same theme.
Zafer is washing my shirts in stonebloody twilight
  under the almond trees
and I am thinking of the laundry
  flapping in the breeze from the sea
as something I'll always remember about this village
  even after I've long forgotten the village
and Zafer, Seher and her younger sisters
  and the sad priest, Hüseyn, to whom they're related.
Hüseyn has climbed up into the minaret, a green cap
  on his head, his hands cupped behind his ears
chanting: Allahüekber, Allahüekber,
  God is most great, God is most great . . .
in a way that seems to make the spring darkness
  even more intense
as if it were not intense enough already.
Up in the amphitheater I'm thinking that God
  really is very great
and that Islam is a green cloth
  which mantles the earth in spring
a green cloth with Arabic letters embroidered in gold
and spring flowers sprouting through the stark green
  in spite of everything.
And it saddens me that I'll never understand the writing entirely.
Yet I would like to be buried wrapped in such a cloth
and have the old mayor, Kadir, and his sons Osman

and Muharrem, whose nickname is Skinny
and the priest, Hüseyn, help carry me to my grave.
From here I can just make out the cypress trees
        of the burial ground and the slanting stones
because the waves are breaking whitely in the dark
        a few hundred feet behind them.
But I can see clearly the faces of the Greek statues
lying on the floor of the amphitheater
        among broken friezes that fell long ago
some women whose faces have partly corroded
and whose vacant eye sockets continually stare at me
        in a way that looks evil.
In the darkness of the spring evening
        I suddenly understand the whole of Greek drama
and feel like one of its main characters, burdened by his fate
as opposed to the scattered figures
        that one by one take their seats.
It is the men from the village,
        who take their hashish from their hiding places
and begin to smoke their evening joints,
        while one sings a lament from Adana.
I recognize blind Mehmet, Little Mustafa
        and his brother, Ali TirTir
who wanted to kill me three days ago
        but regrets it now, or so I hope.
They too are related to Zafer and Seher, but how I don't know.
The priest Hüseyn begins his prayer again;
        it sounds louder now that the stars are out.
And the sound blends with the sound of the sea
        and the rustling of the Eucalyptus trees
and I imagine that the scent of the wild spring flowers
        also blends with the sounds
as well as with the gold Arabic letters
        which I don't completely understand
yet describe my life more exactly than my own words.
And if I should ever write a dissertation
it would have to be about the indescribable euphony in
        Suratultakwir the eightyfirst chapter of the Koran
"When the sun ceases to shine and when stars fall down
        and when the mountains blow away

and when the camels ten months pregnant are left unattended,
      and when the wild animals gather together."
The priest Hüseyn recited it to me a month ago
at a wedding where I danced for eighteen hours with the men
while Zafer and Seher were sitting among the women,
      looking at us stealthily from the darkness of their kerchiefs
and I sent Seher a glance that I wouldn't have dared if I'd been sober.
Maybe that was why Ali TirTir wanted to kill me, I don't know.
I am Orpheus here but without his lyre and his social function
one whose clothes are washed by a woman called Zafer
      with eyes that shine black like knives of obsidian
while her daughter, Seher, walks back and forth
      between the well and the house with even blacker eyes
not knowing anything about Danish art or dissertations
and the two other daughters are sleeping in the dark under
      my white shirts which resemble sails that have no function
because neither my person nor my voice
      shall ever move this village from its place.
And while I walk slowly out of the amphitheater
      and in under the trees
I'm thinking just how much I am nobody
      here among these fragrances.
And even while it occurs to me that the flower of Islamic art
      seen from a period of Danish art
is also a monument to my mistakes,
      nobody will sit wailing at my tomb
and nobody will wash my corpse in wine,
      as Omar Khayyam would have liked to have it.
No matter how intense a spring evening becomes,
      nobody will wrap me in a green cloth
embroidered with gold Arabic letters and carry me to my grave.
Besides that was all long ago and the old mayor is long dead.
His sons, Osman and Muharrem, have become
      corrupt politicians in Ankara.
The priest Hüseyn has moved to a city whose name I have forgotten
along with blind Mehmet, Little Mustafa and his whole family.
Ali TirTir has gone to Europe, Zafer has become old and lame
and Seher has married an engineer called Turgut
from Kayseri, which has nothing at all to do with the story
any more than the fact that Zafer means victory

and Seher dawn, especially in the evening
when I sit here discovering that I have loved you for a week
and it's snowing outside
while you are writing your dissertation on Danish art.

AUTHOR'S AFTERWORD

First of all, let me simply give my heartfelt thanks to Nadia Christensen, who for years has been working at translating my poetry. Her work has been characterized by great skill, deep understanding, and creative faithfulness to the original texts.

The present selection is a result of collaboration between Alexander Taylor and me. It consists partly of older translations by Nadia Christensen or Nadia Christensen and Alexander Taylor, and partly of the translations which Alexander Taylor and I made together in Willimantic from July 29, 1977 to August 7, 1977. I am pleased to say that never in my whole life have I experienced a better collaboration. We have revised several of the poems radically in the process of translating them. We hope that these changes have made the English versions of the poems more effective. It is superfluous to say that only our unusually fine cooperation made these revisions possible. Our aim was to capture the tone and nuances of the original poems rather than be bound by literal translation.

I want to thank Judy Ayer; my wife, Anneli Fuchs; and Patricia Taylor for their warm encouragement, practical help, and useful textual suggestions.

—Henrik Nordbrandt